BELOVED

POEMS BY
FRANCIS C. GRAY

ST. AUGUSTINE'S PRESS
SOUTH BEND, INDIANA

ACKNOWLEDGEMENTS:

"ABC ACROSTIC" AND "JUDAS"
WERE PREVIOUSLY PUBLISHED IN *THE LIVING CHURCH*

"GOD SAT DOWN"
PREVIOUSLY PUBLISHED IN *DIOCESE*

EDITORS: KAREN GRAY AND MATTHEW BORDEN
BOOK DESIGN: DIANN NELSON
COVER DESIGN: DON NELSON

FOR
KATY AND LIBBY AND TIMOTHY
WITH LOVE

PSALM 144:12

TABLE OF CONTENTS

BELOVED

When in that bed you know me almost gone,
where all my mind seems empty to your sight,
remember this, my love, and sing our song
and read my soul away into the night.
In stillness from the place where death attends
will come this antiphon, though not in word
but from the heart; love will make amends.
For voiceless love calls love and thus is heard.
So, I will find release to holy ground
where you are not as yet allowed to be -
carried by your voice and by the sound
of Psalter, Robert Frost, or Emily.
Please do not forget to promise this:
A prayer, a poem, your voice, and last, a kiss.

These sentinels of time in clusters come
together pressed as if proximity
had bound each sender to the other ones.
And I, who lift them from the post, connect
the ancient Portland widow to the rest.
She once asked help, repaying kindness with
now ten December cards. Her grandchildren,
un-met by me, grow, captain swimming teams.
They marry well, not knowing their success
will stoke an evening fire. Her offering
lies by the card postmarked from Florida;
the sender, my dead brother's youthful wife
with whom I waited nightly, knowing death
would not forestall its coming after all.
No letter marks this year for her; we talk
too frequently for that, and well I know
her child grows, fatherless except for God.
The obligation cards in torrents come:
the cleaners, druggist, automotive shop.
The elegiac scrawl of Aunt Virginia,
a lilliputian calendar from church
together come. They bring a welcome close:
the day for which the weary postman waits,
and so do I - the Lord's Nativity.

I asked God for a poem
and for a season
He was quiet,
knowing that my discontent
was not fit vessel
for His prize.
Then one day my neighbor
the angel came whispering,
"He is here."
His presence cleansed the chalice
of my cluttered soul.
I was bare,
and seasons passed before me,
winds before his cave
with voices small,
until that one brief whisper
caught me very unaware.
"I am He."

"I am He saluting you from,
the telescope.
I am He catching your eye
in the microscopic world.
I am He glowing in your chest
when in your joy
you cry alone.
I am He in word made flesh,
in blood stained cup
and broken bread.

I was there when deep within
your mother's womb
you first moved.

I was there when your father
　　　threw up the seed
　　　　　my image made.
I was there in the comfort of your wife
　　　when you in broodings
　　　　　locked your soul.

You asked me for a poem
　　　and I richly supplied
　　　　　lexicons of words,
but you in self-sufficient pride
　　　would only ask, unwilling
　　　　　to explore within.

And so I gave you utterances
　　　in form and meter
　　　　　as you asked.
But they were dust and ashes
　　　for neither you nor I
　　　　　lived in them."

A thousand words God said
　　　and borrowed a second
　　　　　of my time,
and when He left - to stay forever
　　　in my heart's temple -
　　　　　I said, "Amen."

When dying mother said:
"You'll win The Nobel,"
I, Sarah-like,
snickered
in the kitchen of my mind,
thinking her late
to birth a genius
after years of barrenness.
Now I have traded
the hope of being
a reliever
for the Cubbies,
for the numeric cipher
of one ISBN
which identifies
poetic lines, well set.
Thank you for your
dying interest,
Mother.

Yesterday you came to me
      across the tracks of my mind
And led me wandering through the
      parked cars and pennant vendors
to the door of the great coliseum,
      where Jackie Robinson drew a
      base on balls,
and peanuts snapped beneath our feet.

Now the grass leaps from your breast
      growing four seasons
      from your last breath.

Today Jesus gleams with pride
      as his father speaks through
the cloud to explain the kingdom come.
      How nice of God to spend time with
      his son.

Yesterday Timothy received a string of
      ink
Which, tied in knots, said Henry Aaron.
I filed this fragment alphabetically -
      before the boxcars we used to count
and after the ache of knowing
      the caboose is passed.

Fear was the dark friend
with whom my soul kept company those years.
Always he drew close on strange schoolyards,
hovering over this new boy whose dread
of taunt and fist stayed by myself with fear.

He never let me stray.
Fear kept company as parents fought
in dead of night. Urgent accusations,
boozily disclaimed, and muffled by
walls which separated them from me.

Fear attended doorways
while I strayed to see cascading bombs
destroy the Asian city of my birth.
These messengers of death were feeding fear,
bonding me to my companion's side.

He never let me stray.
Fear guided me down corridors of youth,
insuring all the doors of hope stayed closed,
while walking past the rooms where joy and love
taught classes not for me to enter there.

Now fear must go.
For long before he cossetted himself
there was a stronger and more welcome guest,
as fresh as Galilean springtime rain,
older than the morning star at dawn.

Now comes Grace to live.
Long a stranger to my waking self, He
sights the blindness, speaks my silent tongue
and brings to hearing sounds which fear held still,
while corridors long dark are brightening now.

The room is swept.
Candles light the way for love to see
the coming of my lord to Easter dawn,
arrayed not in a tattered cloak of death,
but filled with light which comes beyond the grave
to banish fear.

Seventy-five c.c.'s
of gas-driven pleasure in
red, and made for
slightly less than
my two-twenty body,
lurches into motion
as I take her for a spin.
"F'Chris' sake, you're
fifty-four years old!"
"It's only a test drive,"
I respond, hoping for sympathy,
getting laughter.
"You should ride so well,"
- my retort -
mental, of course,
as the "Esprit" and I
sputter back to her
present owner
whose ten-word ad
could not renew youth after all.
"Caveat Emptor."

I nervously prepare to teach, O God,
the prayer which came intact from Jesus' breath;
trusting my own bread, which seems as odd
as offering croissants to one near death.
Would you in goodness grant the daily crumb,
tomorrow's word impressed with this ink pen,
to free the mind of one poor scribe made numb?
So make this talk of God and not of men.
They are your people after all, your seed;
yours to multiply both bread and word.
Yours the call for me to teach and lead.
Be close by what is spoken, what is heard.
        God, grant me grace to lean upon your staff,
        and give to them your wheat; remove my chaff.

J ust yesterday I knew
E ach breath I ever drew
S ustained by love from you
U ntil life's walk is done
S hall be my victory won.

C ome now, today, and be
H elper and friend to me.
R enew my strength to see
I n you I will be free.
S tay all my fears unknown.
T ake me to be your own.

L ife's tomorrows all will mend
O r else will truly end
R esplendent in your sight.
D eath brings the truest light.

Homilies written
On Pentecost
Leave me
Yet unmoved.

Send thy
Presence to
Invalidate my
Resisting logic:
Invite Grace
To reign.

Catch my
Offending pen and
Make this study
End!

TO A GRANDMOTHER ON HER SECOND WEDDING DAY

For years, you heard love
through the patter of
third generational feet
crossing the sidewalk
of your soul,
vacating lonely places
long unexplored.
Then came love striding soundlessly
on soft mown grass
stealing into chambers
of the soul
where closed doors opened
for springtime
in the afternoon of life.

This is my place.

Here I

hasten to

hear from,

be with,

the inner source

of my being.

Here I am

what I am.

This is where

I am me, and

He enjoys my company.

G od, where are you?

O h yes, I forgot.

D id I not know

C reatures move, not you?

O f course, I drifted.

M y mind cannot hold

E very thought. I slide

B ack to the beginning

A nd become impatient again.

C ome back. I now

K now I was moved.

The news came drifting from cabins
redolent with the unworked
sweat of fourteen-year-old boys.
A dime would change hands,
travelling from expectation
to greed, and coaxing other coin
as wager on the appearance of genitalia.
Laughter ran in nervous bursts,
far too irregular for sanctity,
as arousal edged its way
through puberty.

The dimes and quarters marked the passage
out of Eden, as guilt tiptoed
from between the bunks.
Expectation of trouble loitered in the air.

The girls, for once
knew nothing;
nor did the blood moon speak
upon its rising, to mark
the end of summer.

The time is now
     for the trees to shed their
         vestments
     and cover the ground with
         their raiment.
Earth to earth,
Ashes to ashes,
    as this blanket
    is burned -
    smoldering flame,
    pungent smoke.

The old man, too, is nearing
    the time to discard
        his outer garment -
        earth to earth,
        ashes to ashes,
        dust to dust, and
        lest we forget,
        light to light.

You wait for your daughter - late
returning from a trip
a continent away.
And you say,
in that post-Christian way,
an accident has found her.
If this were just a date,
a night out on the town,
an evening say
of local play,
then at least today -
Wait, an engine stops.
A slamming door
three hours late,
but what's a wait?
That's what a father's for.

We timidly approach this man of power
whose very voice brings down a city wall.
We offer him remainders of our trip
lest he ask much. Our vinegar for wine,
the moldy bread to feign a longer trip;
our disguise, a skin of lies adorned
with tattered rags from beggars at the gate.
We dare not speak as vigorous men, or else
his trumpet sound will slice through city walls
singing the song of death. Swiftly he rides
and death is ours unless we swallow pride
and thus avoid this nearest neighbor's sword.
"Give to us now a promise of surcease
to quell the apprehension of our lives,
for without covenant we die nearby."
The taste of grovel settles in the throat
much easier when laced with honeyed guile.
Our future? Life in some reduced estate,
yet life itself was all we had to save.

Joshua 9:3-18

CINQUAINS

A BAKER'S DOZEN

In the
Beginning, God!
(All else, parenthetic.)
The word was with God, begotten
not made.

Genesis 1:1

John 1:1

Golden,
the valley calf.
A mountain God brings wrath.
Who sheaths the sword of God's judgment?
Moses.

The road
Angelically
Narrowed and I lay down.
You struck and cursed. Now who is the
Donkey?

Numbers 22: 23-35

Swiftly
my stalking horse
traverses the kingdom,
trampling dissent, even mine.
Joab.

2 Samuel 19:5

J ourney!
O n the way to
N owhere, I was eaten
A live. Lord, I give up. Please, whale,
H url me.

Jonah 2

B efore
I ncarnation
R umors of angels spread
T hat mangers would tabernacle
H eaven.

Abba,
deodorize
the room of my spirit.
Invade the shade, under my tree
to dwell.

Jonah 4:5

Abba
- child to parent.
Jesus said you listen.
Close as mother's breast, father's lap.
Abba

Seeing
the baby, my
dream fulfilled in one glance.
Your glory shines. Could I now be
dismissed?

Luke 2:25-32

Merchant,
you know my worth.
I am yours to purchase;
costing you a lifetime, I am
the pearl.

P utting
E ffort into
T alk by the fireside
E ntrapped this large Galilean.
R ock? Not!

Matthew 26: 69-75

Gardener,
you stole his voice.
Where have you put my Lord?
Only one says "Mary" that way -
Rabbi?

John 20: 14-18

The soul -
a coracle
on a dangerous sea,
oarless, until apprehended
by grace!

TREASURE

The treasure in the field once lay
for hand to touch and eye behold;
for any one with willing feet
to walk the ground, the prize unfold.
Then tractors gutted loam and grass,
roiling the green in tattered shreds.
Loaded trucks were made to pass
down thoroughfares to dumping beds.
The treasure was not found nor sought.
It disappeared without a trace
as other vehicles were brought
to cover earth with concrete base.
   So the prize was never found.
   The treasure was the field, the ground.

There went a wife and man
to be enrolled at census time;
hers, the weight of glory,
his, the burden of the world.
There she was delivered
where wood encradled straw.
To that portal
we, too, come to be enrolled
at birthing time.

The pocket hole
through which I slid
neglected to inform
the landlord of the trousers
of my escape.
The crack I snuggled into
offered no resistance.
The broom, however,
vigilant in the arms
of my owner's wife
restored me triumphantly
to her purse, not his.
Small that I am,
I am a joy to her
and to her son
who told of me,
likening me to the kingdom.
As one who was found,
I am a treasure.

Yesterday, he found her unsuspecting,
    resting in beauty,
    verdant, content, drinking air and soil.

Unlike others who passed, he spoke.
    She listened for expectant blessings
    from the quieter of lakes,
    harvester of fish,
    multiplier of bread.

Lilies sang his love,
    soil whispered generosity,
    storms rumbled his power.

Yet, his words breathed flame -
    scorching bark, bubbling sap
    long languid in her veins.

He looked beyond the seasons,
    saw the sloth,
    smote those branches,
    parched her farthest roots,
    and her heart was melting wax.

Today, in returning,
    people cringed to see her
    withered at his decree,
    dried up as a potsherd,
    cleaving to the rock.

May a remembrance be her issue,
    instead of fruit, for
    she was consumed by his zeal.

I came from Egypt, camel borne,

    caprisoned in this jar -

    a thousand flowers pressed for me;

    a family laboring a year

    to fashion earth, wind, rain and sun

    to perfume just one ear.

A Galilean foot was not

    receptacle for all of me,

    but years of use, drop by drop.

    The girl poured all

    and did not stop.

    I owned the air inside that hall.

Thus, I upon his body lay

    and came by foot on Easter Day.

John 12:1-11

Fault me not
    as Satan's way
        into the traitor's soul.
The Lord, he tore
    me from the loaf
        and gave me to him whole.
But I believe
    that darkness lurked
        before he ate and drank.
I was but sign,
    not sacrament,
        of evil in the rank.
Think me not
    as Judas' sign
        to leave and cut his deal.
Connect me with
    the larger loaf
        of Eucharistic meal.

John 13:26

I was darkness, with ears alert
and a tasting tongue.
The ways of compensation for the blind
lighted my path.
The breath of wool
wafting from new garments
informed me of wealth
approaching my waystation.

Conversations a league removed
included me as I waited
for pause to make my pitch.
As footsteps receded,
dust swirled, muffling words
as I turned for the next approach.

Once - and only once -
a voice so clear caused light
behind my eyelids, and I cried.
Moving granite sounded no lower,
nor crystal more clear than his voice.
"Rabbi," said I,
followed more insistently
by shrieks of desperation
as Light approached with every step.

They tried to still me -
those Galilean clods
who stunk of fish,
who spoke the thick Northern tongue.

But I was louder still,
for Light approached
and darkness no longer became me.

"What do you want?" the granite spoke,
as beams bounced and pinged
inside my shell, demanding freedom.
"That I might see, Rabbi."
"Be it so." And darkness fled.

A cascade flowed of tears
taking darkness down my cheek
as first I saw his face,
touched his hand,
smelled wood shavings,
and heard the laugh
to silence angels.

He no longer comes this way, to Jericho.
Jerusalem took him,
for it claims all prophets.
But, on occasion, his fishermen
pass this town with eyes like his
to greet me as a brother.
They, too, have come from blindness,
and welcome the sight of another
who has eyes to see.

Mark 10:46-52

Just as I am
Under this branch
Dying in
Asphyxiation.
Save me, Lord.

Mary did not get to touch,
      but loved in such
completeness that the simple
      non-ascended no
was all sufficient for her gaze.

Thomas was so near
      of sight and spoke
for ages yet to come
      and had to touch and plunge
perhaps as much with shame as wonder.

Peter, blunt of word and
      quick of hand in net and sail
had need of broiled fish as redness
      slipping through charcoal
anointed his inner flame.

And so to those he loved in flesh
      he reappeared in deed, as well,
And showed that death
      could not take away the touch
and taste and vision which
      the Father had transformed
          with wood and iron.

Then came angels

       unearthing dead things

Like the Counselor

       who took the secret

And breathed chalky embers

       into flames.

When tombs are opened

       fresh air goes in.

The spirits emerge

       and Christ lives.

AN ICE LADEN TREE ON ASH WEDNESDAY

In greyness sits this rime encrusted tree
protected from the cold, yet colder still.
Wrapped in beauty, shrouded by the chill,
it cannot thaw until light sets it free.
The darkness of the overhanging sky
forbids the climbing sun to melt the ice,
holding the shimmering sparkle, freezing thrice -
the tree, the ground, the wind with shiver sigh.
Come, Lord, and melt my glitter casing time.
Come thaw this heart with radiant love of thee.
Unbind the twig, branch, trunk and all the tree
to loose this heart from prose to Easter rhyme.
      That with your spring this Lenten soul might bloom.
      Thus grace come forth and greyness stay in tomb.

Alone
Before the world's
Conception, God, you
Drew plans for
Eons on nothing
Firmer than emptiness.
Galaxies expanded from
Holes blacker than
Ink, as you
Joined two molecules
Kindling in them
Life.
More
Neutrons and protons
Ordered into existence,
Poured from your
Quintessential being, to
Roil this planet,
Sending capillary signals -
Taking flesh in
Universe of bodies
Variant as bees,
Whales, humans. Yes,
Xenogenetic was
Your
Zeal!

Rules of engagement state, one must not kill
a naked soldier while he takes a shower;
as undefended and against his will
without his clothes, he seems to lose his power.
Such intercourse among the warrior caste
was held unwritten law for centuries.
This courtesy has, lately, not held fast
for slaughters now are frequent as the breeze.
In God's command the opposite is right.
His undressed troops are martyred, year by year.
The Innocents of Bethlehem by night;
by day his unclothed son is pierced with spear.
      In paradise God's holy ones will be
      standing, clothed, in their right mind, as He.

Stormy sea, troubled me,
quiet lake, rest to take.
Pausing on the gentle hill,
Mountains pushing to the sea,
soil cleared, prepared to till,
panorama made for me.

Heavy heat, wish for sleep,
many talks, longer walks.
Were disciples skipping stones
idly as he spoke so clear,
and did their minds fail to contain
just as mine as I sit here?

When in mystery the great
I am called Moses out,
Little did he know
Like-minded men for ages
Into eternity would
Answer - stammering or bold,
My will is Yours.

For all of them and
One in particular may the
Lord be praised. That one, your
Well beloved son, new
Exodus from pain to joy.
Let us our orders all fulfill -
Loving, gracious, stalwart, still.

She sucked her bottom lip
    and gazed up for yes,
        down for no.
The room was so still,
    the nurse had left,
        we were alone.
I grasped for comfort words
    and searched my heart
        for His words.
But I was so complex
    and she so simple,
        no spark came.
I spoke of grevious sin.
    The eyes were dull,
        down for no.
I mentioned deep tormented pain.
    She loosed the lip
        and gazed up.
Blessed the pure in heart
    I thought, and prayed
        for more words.
The ones God makes free
    are free, in heaven.
        The eyes arise.
And so that still afternoon
    loosing came from heaven.
        Eyes up - yes.
No words came
    but her eyes spoke.

I am
toiling and spinning
incessantly without the
glory of those lilies.
       They wasted time -
sat
       basked
              drank dew
                    and did not move
                        as I.

Yet -
I am his clothing
too.

Arriving at the window
    later in the day,
    the sun offers light,
    guardedly; husbanding his gift
    as if preparing for a drought.

Somewhere another leaf
    releases its hold.
The grey heron rises
    as winter begins.
October's moon prepares
    to refute the sun:
    her own light
    his borrowed gift.

The slate sky will pour forth
Only sleet and snow
Upon the bosom of our souls
Until the Son melts our hardness.
When we are thawed, the dead fish
Tossed on our shore in the storms of fall
Will become the loam of our fields.
The lenten land will flower
Only at his bidding
When we have quit the fight.
Easter will steal upon us
As we walk in his new garden
For we will know him.

Kairos came and snuggled

between a clock

and me, telling

me it was

hitime

to

invest

in an alarm

to awaken me.

Kairos is so slim; a

glassy space from here to there.